WISE
BEFORE THE
EVENT

Coping with crises in schools

by William Yule
and Anne Gold

Published by
Calouste Gulbenkian Foundation
London 1993

William Yule trained as a clinical psychologist and spent six years in educational and epidemiological research before returning to the staff at the Institute of Psychiatry where he is Professor of Applied Child Psychology and head of the clinical psychology services. He has published 300 articles and 9 books on a wide range of topics in child psychology such as autism, the use of behavioural techniques by parents and teachers, the effects of lead on children's development and children's fears. Since the capsize of the cross-channel car ferry,'Herald of Free Enterprise', in 1987 he has been very involved in the study and treatment of Post Traumatic Stress Disorder in adults and children.

Anne Gold taught in Inner London comprehensive schools for 20 years. She was head of a Special Educational Needs Department and then a pastoral head. She is now a lecturer in the Management Development Centre at the University of London, Institute of Education, where she works closely with schools and teachers on managing their institutions.

Contents

Foreword

Disasters happen frequently and sometimes their victims are school children; consequently the schools they attend may be affected in a number of ways. For example, if a pupil dies the whole school may feel the loss; or, when pupils who have suffered shock or injury return to school they may need to be treated with particular sensitivity. There are any number of possibilities requiring any number of responses. Although a proportion of schools will have some idea of what these responses should be, many will not.

Schools are very busy places and to give consideration to how they might react in the event of a disaster that has yet to happen is unlikely to be a priority. Nor is it an appealing prospect and the two may not be unconnected. It is also true that schools, like the rest of us, are inclined to believe that disasters will always strike elsewhere. However, as the newspapers repeatedly testify, schools often have to cope with crises. How they do this, once the spotlight of publicity has moved on, is less clear but it is likely that many will improvise. Sometimes this will suffice; sometimes mistakes may be made which could have been avoided, or sensibilities damaged that are particularly exposed.

The purpose of this booklet is to assist teachers in such circumstances and to encourage them to think ahead. It aims to raise awareness of the possible effects of disasters on school children, as well as the life of the school, and to suggest ways in which advance planning can reduce their impact. The word 'school' here refers to primary and secondary schools, mainstream and special. While the booklet is aimed chiefly at staff and governors, we hope that parents also may find some of the material useful.

Simon Richey
Assistant Director, Education
Calouste Gulbenkian Foundation, UK Branch

Acknowledgements

The authors would like to thank Elizabeth Jones HMI and Simon Richey (Assistant Director, Education, at the Calouste Gulbenkian Foundation UK Branch) for their continuous support and guidance; also, grateful thanks to Jeremy Caddy (Head Teacher, Greenham Court County Primary School, Berkshire), Elizabeth Capewell (Director, Centre for Crisis Management and Education), Karen Dagwell (Deputy Head Teacher, Sydenham School, London Borough of Lewisham), Beverley Hamilton (Senior Teacher, Whitefield School, London Borough of Barnet), and Elizabeth Monck (Senior Research Fellow, Institute of Child Health) for commenting so helpfully on the text.

Introduction

Shortly after school started on the morning of 21st October 1966, a huge coal tip slid down a mountain side in Wales and engulfed the primary school in Aberfan, killing 116 children and 28 adults. One hundred and forty three primary school children survived. Scarcely a family in this tightly-knit community escaped the disaster.

Contemporary reports describe how many of the surviving children developed difficulties going to sleep, became nervous and were unwilling to go to school. Some had nightmares, others started to wet their beds. Bad weather, of the sort that had preceded the disaster, made them more nervous. But few children spoke spontaneously of their experiences.

Twenty two years later to the day, on the 21st October 1988, the cruise ship 'Jupiter' sailed from Athens to take a party of some 400 British school children and their teachers on an educational trip of the Eastern Mediterranean. A short distance from Piraeus harbour, the 'Jupiter' was struck amidships and holed by an Italian tanker. The ship began to list and sank within 45 minutes. Although only one teacher and one pupil were missing, presumed drowned, two rescuers were killed and many children saw their bodies. The children were flown home the following day to a barrage of publicity.

Schools varied greatly in how they dealt with the aftermath of the 'Jupiter' sinking. Some were very sympathetic and arranged individual and group help; others wanted to forget the whole episode and discouraged children from even talking about it.

How would your school have responded to such an event? What would you have said to worried parents before they knew their children were safe? What changes might you expect in the children's behaviour? How would you prepare teachers to discuss the incident in the classroom? Should you mention it at assembly?

Should you hold a memorial service? What would you do about the next school journey?

In the 22 years between the tragedy of Aberfan and the sinking of the 'Jupiter', it appeared that very little had been learnt about ways of helping schools come to terms with the aftermath of such disasters. However, since the spate of disasters that affected Britain in the late 1980s, such as the fire at Bradford and the crush at Hillsborough football ground, more has been understood about the longer-term consequences of disasters on individuals and communities, and about the ways that some of these can be mitigated.

If such incidents as those described above are rare, there are nonetheless many other traumas that may affect schools, as a recent cutting from *The Guardian* (right) illustrates.

While large-scale disasters may happen infrequently, small-scale incidents happen with far greater frequency. Regardless of the size

cases for the head

1. April 1991: 15-year-old boy expelled from Milton Abbey School, Dorset after discovery of sawn-off shotgun, crossbow and machetes.
2. March 1991: 15-year-old boy charged with attempted murder after shooting teacher at Colston's School, Bristol.
3. January 1991: Two boys, 14 and 15, jailed after burning down Maiden Erleigh School, Reading.
4. May 1990: Four-year-old boy removed by police from Sparkenhoe Primary School, Leicester after "damaging at least three children".
5. June 1988: 16-year-old boy jailed for life after injuring a teacher and two pupils at Higham Ferrers School, Northampton with shotgun.
6. September 1987: 15-year-old sentenced to seven years for attacking deputy head of Priory School, Liverpool.
7. May 1985: Four boys expelled and 10 suspended from Uppingham School, Leicestershire after drunken rampage.

First published in The Guardian 3 May 1991

of the incident, the distress caused to the individuals involved can be equally devastating.

No-one can predict when a disaster will occur; and thinking ahead and planning will not *make* the disaster happen. Forward planning, however, may help a school to cope better after a disaster, and it may well help reduce the distress of young people and staff.

The text starts with five short case studies which illustrate ways in which children, as well as adults, react to life-threatening events. It describes their various stress reactions and shows how these interfere with adjustment and attainment in school. Then it considers how schools can plan ahead in the short, medium and longer-term so that when, and if, a disaster strikes, however large or small, staff and parents are better prepared to cope with its effects.

DISASTERS AND THEIR EFFECTS

Staff need to be aware of the types of crises that may affect schools. Pupils may be affected by crises that occur either in or out of school. Here are some examples:

In-school

- the death of a pupil or member of staff through natural causes, such as illness;
- a traffic accident involving a pupil or staff member;
- a deliberate act of violence, such as a knifing or the use of a firearm;
- a school fire or an explosion in a laboratory

Out-of-school

- deaths or injuries on school journeys (for example, the children who were swept out to sea at Lands End, or the children involved in the sinking of the 'Jupiter');
- tragedies involving children from many schools such as the fire at the Bradford football stadium; the crush at Hillsborough football ground; the sinking of the 'Herald of Free Enterprise'; and the devastation at Lockerbie following the Pan Am explosion;
- civil disturbances involving bombs such as in Northern Ireland;
- refugee children joining a school, uprooted from their countries and perhaps shocked by wars or atrocities

The emotional effects of disasters on children are not always immediately obvious to parents or school staff. Indeed, at times children find it difficult to confide their distress to adults as they know that it will upset them. In some children the distress can last for months, even years, and may also affect their academic attainment.

Schools too can be difficult places in which to express feelings and emotions: while they may be good at celebrating joyful events, often they have more difficulty with feelings of anger or sadness. There are schools where young people do not feel comfortable enough to explore private thoughts in public or with staff as they fear their confidence may be abused. Similarly, because many adults are not able to talk about death, bereavement and tragedy, they may unwittingly stop children talking about similar emotional experiences.

A school which has thought seriously about issues, such as confidentiality, and has made plans within the curriculum to explore such matters as birth and death, will be more open to exploring difficult feelings. This in turn might better prepare staff to cope with the range and complexity of feelings that a crisis can engender.

Five case examples

In recent years a great deal has been learned about the effects that life-threatening traumas have on adult survivors. Children too are affected emotionally. For a long time adults assumed that these effects were short-lived but since sympathetic professionals began to ask the children themselves how they were affected, it transpired that they showed a similar range of difficulties to adults.

The following case examples drawn from clinical practice illustrate the range of traumas that school children may encounter; the ways that some schools have reacted; and the different types of emotional, behavioural and learning problems experienced by the children themselves.

1 Survivors of the 'Herald of Free Enterprise'

An eight year-old boy was physically unharmed when the 'Herald of Free Enterprise' capsized. He quickly learned not to discuss his emotional reactions for fear of upsetting adults. Thus, neither his parents nor school staff were aware of the extent of his suffering.

Bill had gone on the day trip to Belgium with his parents and elder sister to practise crossing in a ferry as they feared he might not be a good traveller. Otherwise, he was a well-adjusted eight year-old. Bill was standing by the table near the cafeteria just as the boat shuddered and cups started to slip off the table. His father grabbed his arm and held him as the boat keeled over. As the water started to rise, his father helped him climb the sides of the now vertical tables. His mother was trapped in the water. When the helicopters arrived and ropes were lowered through the smashed portholes, the children were got out first and therefore separated from their parents. They

3

were not reunited until all were on dry land a few hours later. Fortunately Bill and his family survived. They were flown home the following day.

For the first three weeks at home all the family were very distressed. They wanted to be close together initially, but after three days Bill was returned to school as his constant questioning and distress were too difficult for his mother to cope with: uncharacteristically, he was perpetually on the move, snatching things, fiddling with things, not doing as he was asked, making noises, and generally being disruptive and defiant. His sleep was disrupted. He had frightening dreams of the boat going over and would regularly go into his parents' room to sleep in their bed. At school he had great difficulty in concentrating, didn't listen to teachers and couldn't answer questions.

Nearly three months after the accident, he was downstairs on a double decker bus going to a football match when the bus swayed as it went round a roundabout. He shouted, *"It's going over, Dad!"*, and had to be taken off the bus as he was so terrified. When interviewed alone, he confided, *"Sometimes when I am in my classroom, and I am standing over my desk, I think the room is going to go over. At night, I often dream that the world is going over on its side, all the people will go in the air, up in the sky, and all will get separated"*. Neither Bill's parents nor teachers had reported any significant level of disturbance. Nonetheless, he was diagnosed as suffering from Post Traumatic Stress Disorder (PTSD), a condition we shall discuss later.

Bill joined a group with other child and adolescent survivors to talk through his reactions. At one point he suddenly broke down into inconsolable tears. He said that he was being teased at school by another child who said such things as *"I wish you had died on the Ferry"*. The others were asked how he should deal with this. An older girl who had lost both parents on the ferry said that she too had been teased at school and called 'orphan'. It had hurt her tremendously, but she knew that she had to ignore it. The therapist said that while this was hard, but right for her, it could not be expected that the younger child should do so. The group agreed that the therapist had to ask the boy's parents to intervene and talk to the head teacher, and that this was not 'telling tales'. The parents told the head who dealt with it promptly. Nonetheless, neither the parents nor the teachers had known about the teasing and its effects on the boy.

This next example illustrates the added complications of physical injury and bereavement

Mary, aged 13, was sitting in the cafeteria of the 'Herald of Free Enterprise' with her parents and a friend when the boat went over. She and her mother were catapulted out of their seats, across the room, and smashed through a glass partition. Mary remembers being close to her mother in the water in the dark with all the noise around. She must have been close to her mother when her mother drowned, but she cannot recall any details after reaching the water where she remained for over two hours. She was in hospital in Belgium for a few weeks recovering from her injuries.

Once home she found it very difficult to talk to her father or siblings about her experiences, but spent hours obsessionally discussing it with her friend. She was very upset by references to the disaster made at school. She was totally unable to concentrate on school work. She found great difficulty getting to sleep at night. She had worries about travelling by ferry or aeroplane. She needed to be out of the house, seeking her friends' company. She suffered flashbacks, especially re-hearing the sound of breaking glass.

Mary had to cope with the feelings of the loss of her mother. She had not been able to attend the funeral as she was still in hospital, and so could not say goodbye to her mother. Once home, her schooling was disrupted further by many hospital appointments. Her father's own grief prevented him from comforting her. It was many months before professional help was organised for her.

Most children find it difficult to concentrate following a disaster, which consequently affects their school work. Exam preparation and standards of achievement may suffer unless the problem is recognised

John was nearly 16 when he accompanied his parents and elder brother on the day trip to Belgium. He should have been in school; so, in order to salve his conscience a little, he took his GCSE English course work with him to prepare for the exam. Fortunately, when the ship capsized, all his family survived...but not the English course work.

Back home he had tremendous difficulties getting to sleep. He could not discuss the accident with his parents as they were still too upset. He was tired and could not concentrate in school or revise at home. Months later it emerged in a group session that the teachers were not only pressurising him to keep up-to-date with his preparation for GCSE but were also expecting him to re-write all the course work destroyed in the accident (the GCSE had just been introduced and teachers and pupils alike were under pressure). Once the problem was acknowledged, a brief discussion with the teachers resulted in rescheduling his revision and a letter being sent to the examining board to explain the unusual circumstances. John felt that the burden had been lifted and was better able to concentrate.

2 The 'Jupiter' cruise sinking

In the 'Herald of Free Enterprise' disaster, most of the surviving children were unknown to each other: up to 25 schools had only one affected pupil to care for. This made for difficulties in getting an adequate picture of what the children had actually experienced and in recognising that much of their behaviour was indeed reaction to their experience. In contrast, when the 'Jupiter' sank, about 20 schools each had up to 30 pupils on board. One school had to cope with the death of one pupil; another school had to adjust to the death of a teacher. Most, like the school in the next example, had to try to understand the reactions of a very traumatised group of teenagers. This section therefore illustrates the effects of a disaster on a whole school, as opposed to the previous example which described the effects on individuals.

As the ship left Piraeus harbour it was beginning to get dark. Some of the groups of pupils were lining up for the evening meal, some were attending a briefing lecture on what they were to see on the trip.

At first, when the collision occurred, no one realised the seriousness of the situation. Very quickly the 'Jupiter' shipped water and began listing to port and aft. Children were told to assemble in a lounge on an upper deck, but many were unfamiliar with the layout of the ship. As the vessel listed at 45° and then worse, they found it very difficult to get around. Children became separated from friends and teachers. Many were able to jump across to tugs that had come alongside, but two seamen assisting in the transfer were fatally crushed between the ship and the tug: many children saw their dead bodies.

Other children, some of whom were non-swimmers, clung to the railings on the topmost deck under the lifeboats and had to jump into the water as the 'Jupiter' went down, its funnel hissing and spurting out soot and smoke. Children and staff in the dark clung to wreckage in the oily water until rescued. Some of those who were swimming were terrified that they would be run down by the rescue craft. It was many hours before it was realised that all but one child and one teacher had survived. After spending a sleepless night on a sister ship moored in Piraeus harbour, the children were flown home to a barrage of publicity.

Some reactions in school

In one of the schools, a girls' school, the staff invited psychologists in during a Staff Development Day. The psychologists met the teachers who had led the trip, girls who had survived and most of the parents. This initial, marathon meeting permitted the girls to discuss their feelings both at home and at school.

Over the next few weeks there were many incidents of girls getting very upset and having to leave the classroom. Arrangements were made for making this as easy as possible and for the head of year to be informed. Such incidents were regularly reviewed with the psychologists when they visited the school.

Even the most experienced teacher can be caught on the hop. A minor and apparently unconnected incident can trigger off a major reaction. For instance, it was an unfortunate coincidence that when survivors went in to the geography class it still had a display on the subject of 'Great Disasters of the World'. Once the girls could see what was triggering off their distress they were far better able to cope.

In some cases it took longer to spot the connections. One girl got very upset and felt that staff were not caring about her (although this was far from the truth). She cited as an example that she had come in late one wet day and the class teacher had ignored her. It turned out that while sitting in her wet clothes she felt just as she had done on the quayside at Piraeus. It took a long time to convince her that perhaps she should have taken some responsibility herself and told the class teacher, who, after all, could hardly have read her mind.

Things settled down in that particular school over the next two terms. Then a number of girls in the fifth form experienced an upsurge of difficulties going into assembly, having been able to stand the crowds before the summer break. Careful questioning revealed that one of the privileges of being in the fifth year was that these girls could now sit in the balcony during assembly. The balcony was steeply raked and had a small iron hand rail at the bottom of the steps. Unfortunately, this reminded many of them of their ordeal in negotiating the steeply sloping deck of the ship with the iron rails going around the decks. Once this was realised, this problem went away.

Effects on school work

In all the examples so far, the children had difficulties with sleep and with concentration. Inevitably, teachers and parents were worried about the effects on their school performance. Surprisingly, this phenomenon had rarely been studied. The following provides some useful insights.

In one school, the end of year exam results for the three years before the disaster were compared with the end of term results ten months after the sinking. The results can be seen in the graph:

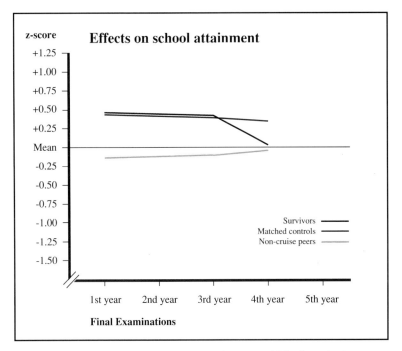

Tsui E, Dagwell K and Yule W (1993) *Effect of a disaster on children's academic attainment* (in preparation)

As can be seen, the girls who went on the cruise were slightly abler than the rest in the fourth year. By comparing them with 24 matched for their levels of achievement prior to the accident, it can be seen that the sinking did indeed have a significant effect on their school performance. This effect persisted through the following year and resulted in lower GCSE results than had been originally predicted. There was a suggestion that the brighter girls seemed to recover sooner than the less so.

▨ The Hillsborough disaster

This example illustrates how, in addition to general support in dealing with a traumatic bereavement, a particular pupil required specialist help to overcome a phobia he had developed.

9

Fourteen year-old Mark went with his mother to see his favourite football team play at Hillsborough. She was crushed to death. He escaped onto the pitch where he saw others die. Later he had to identify his mother from a polaroid photo taken at the scene. For months, in addition to coping with his bereavement, he found that he was irritable at school and got into a great deal more trouble than usual. He also became considerably distressed whenever he heard a word including '...borough' mentioned in any news bulletin or elsewhere.

Mark went through the usual pattern of grief and was greatly supported by a social worker and a teacher in school. Talking over the details of what happened that day helped him deal with his feelings about the accident, but he was left with this marked reaction to 'borough' words. The psychologist treating him made up a tape of hundreds of such words. Mark was taught the rudiments of relaxation and then, when relaxed, he would listen to the tape repeatedly. After a few sessions with the tape, the dreaded word lost its power to raise anxieties and he was able to resume a relatively normal life.

◪ A teacher

Accidents during school journeys affect teachers as well as pupils. This case illustrates how a good teacher, before skilled therapy was arranged, came close to giving up the profession.

Miss Leader was 35 years old and had been teaching in secondary schools for just over 10 years. She was an excellent teacher who had taken many groups of pupils on school journeys. On one trip overseas, the coach in which her group was travelling was involved in a collision. At first it was not clear how many children had been killed because the survivors were dispersed to several local hospitals.

Miss Leader recalls that initially she felt calm and in charge. She did what she could to comfort wounded children and then set about the task of trying to find out if all were safe. She remembers that the worst moment was when she arrived at the first hospital and took out her tattered list containing the names of the children in the party.

"Up until then I had been fairly calm, almost operating on an automatic pilot. But as I ticked the names off my list, suddenly it hit me. How on earth could I tell Mr and Mrs Briggs that Sharon was dead? What about Mrs Hollis who had relied on Gavin since his father died? Every name without a tick meant another set of parents to tell, another funeral to attend. I just knew I couldn't face that. I felt so helpless."

In the event none of her party was badly hurt and all were returned home within a few days. On getting back to school Miss Leader had to tell her story many times, but she never shared her worst fears of feeling so helpless and having to attend the funerals. For the first few weeks she seemed to cope at work, but she had increasing difficulty sleeping. No matter how tired she was, as soon as her head hit the pillow, she kept replaying the scenes of the crash in her head. She grew steadily more tired, more irritable and less able to concentrate. Halfway through the following term she decided to change from full-time to part-time work.

Her colleagues were sympathetic and supportive, but felt out of their depth. Eventually, she saw a nurse therapist who discussed the crash in detail, concentrating on her most private feelings and thoughts about it. As they confronted these fears and feelings, so she overcame them and within two months was fully functioning once more. She still remembers all that happened, but now can control those memories and they no longer upset her.

5 A road traffic accident

When a child dies or is badly hurt in an accident on the way to school, the school has to decide how to respond and what to tell the other children. As the next case illustrates, teachers need to be aware of how being involved in a traumatic death can affect a pupil.

David was 10 when he walked home from school one day with his mother, younger sister and other pupils and their parents. They all walked on the pavement as usual, but this did not save them when a lorry skidded on a wet road, mounted the pavement and ploughed into their party. David's sister and one other pupil were killed, and his mother slightly injured.

This is an all too familiar sad story that can be read daily in a local newspaper. However, the effects on David and the school were devastating. Staff were shocked, but dealt well with the immediate aftermath. They told the children in broad outline what had happened; they helped them to make cards to send to the bereaved families. They were quietly sympathetic as the funerals came and went. They resolved to keep their teaching on road safety high on the agenda.

Meanwhile, David became more tearful and listless. He could not concentrate on his work and often seemed to be day-dreaming. He lost interest in football, something that had been his great passion. One day, as he was on his own in the classroom, he blurted out to his teacher that he had imagined that his mother had been killed in the accident. She listened and took David to a quiet room where he could tell her all that had happened and all that he had feared.

"I was walking on the inside of the pavement, just behind Lisa (his sister). Suddenly, I heard a noise and saw a lorry come up onto the pavement and hit her and mummy. I saw Lisa being crushed and I knew straightaway she was dead. Mummy was knocked over a wall, and she was taken to hospital. I was taken home to a friend's house."

At the time of the incident David had not known whether his mother would live. He had no one with whom to share his reactions after seeing his sister killed. His mother was so obviously upset that he did not want to upset her further by telling her what he had seen.

David needed a sympathetic adult to hear his story in all its gory detail. He needed to make sense of what he saw; to reassure himself that his sister was killed outright; to know that he could have done nothing to prevent the accident; and to share his sense of loss when he thought his mother had also been killed. All were feelings that were too painful to share with his distressed mother. His teacher listened, explained and reassured him. When he was ready, she got him to talk through how he was going to cope without his sister as customary playfellow. She made a note to remember the anniversary of the accident so that she could acknowledge that important date to David and to talk through how he wanted to mark it.

The wide range of these crises, whether affecting one child, one family, one school or a whole community, shows many similarities of response and illustrate a wide range of individual reactions.

Reactions to major stress in adults and young people

Schools need to be aware of the **range** of symptoms (illustrated in the previous section) that both children and teachers may show after a major trauma. The most important thing is for teachers and those who have management responsibility for teachers to note any major change in behaviour after a disaster; to note the nature of those changes; and to alert others as agreed in the school contingency plan (discussed later).

The case examples drew attention to the wide range of reactions shown by children following a variety of traumatic experiences. It is important for parents and teachers to realise that a high proportion of children may experience intense distress and that this may last more than two years in a sizeable minority.

Following the Aberfan disaster, Lacey (1972) described how 56 children reacted over the following four years:

"Symptoms varied but the commonest were sleeping difficulties, nervousness, lack of friends, unwillingness to go to school or out to play, instability and enuresis. Some of the children too had shown some of these symptoms before the disaster, but they were said to be very much worse after it. Broadly speaking, the children who were most affected were those with other anxiety-creating situations in their backgrounds." (Lacey, 1972, p 259)

Some anxious parents became over-protective of their children. Fears of the dark and nightmares caused sleep problems. Bad weather upset the children as a period of bad weather had preceded the tip slide. Children rarely spoke spontaneously of their experiences. Three children played games of 'burying' in the sand.

Where certain symptoms are present the child is likely to be suffering from a syndrome that is now recognised as **Post Traumatic Stress Disorder (PTSD)**.

Post Traumatic Stress Disorder

Post Traumatic Stress Disorder is defined by the World Health Organisation and the American Psychiatric Association as a reaction that may follow an event that is outside the range of usual human experience and would be very distressing to almost anyone.

There are three main groups of symptoms or reactions:

(1) The traumatic event is persistently re-experienced in thoughts, dreams or flashbacks where the individual thinks it is all happening again.

(2) There is persistent avoidance of stimuli associated with the trauma, or there is numbing of general responsiveness.

(3) There are signs of increased physiological arousal such as disturbed sleep and poor concentration.

PTSD is now recognised as a normal reaction to an abnormal situation. Along with that recognition has come improved ways of successfully helping those affected. It is important that people are reassured that, while distressing, the symptoms described here can be treated successfully.

Like most of us, children - especially adolescents - worry that they are going mad when they start experiencing some or many of these symptoms. They need to be reassured that they are not. However, not everyone shows all these responses. There is a wide range of individual reactions. For example, some people get very anxious, phobic about particular objects or situations encountered during a disaster, or become very depressed or suicidal.

In the following section we describe in greater detail the symptoms associated with PTSD, additional reactions to major crises and some of the ways in which individuals and schools can support pupils and their families. Although staff may also develop PTSD, and this needs to be recognised and treated, here we concentrate on the effects on pupils, mainly in the eight to eighteen year range or junior to secondary age.

(1) Re-experiencing the trauma

Most young people are troubled by repetitive, intrusive thoughts about the accident. These may occur at any time, although they are often triggered by something in their environment that reminds them of the accident - for example, as we have seen, children from shipping disasters may get upset by movement on a bus, the noise of glass smashing, the sound of rushing water, the sight of tables laid out like a ship's cafeteria and so forth. Distressing thoughts tend to intrude when the children are otherwise quiet. Sometimes they can have 'flashbacks' as if they were reliving the experience. They may also relive the incident in recurring nightmares.

(2)Avoiding thinking about the experience

The emotions that the intrusive thoughts give rise to can be very painful and often young people try to avoid thinking about the trauma or avoid dealing with the emotions. They may steer clear of things that remind them of the trauma because such things are like powerful fears which actually happen. While in many adults there is evidence of difficulty in sustaining emotional relationships or in having loving feelings, these signs may be different in children. For example, they may often show a lack of interest in hobbies and pastimes previously enjoyed.

The symptoms of this kind of avoidance may appear as:

a. Not talking with parents Many young people do not want to talk about their feelings with their parents so as not to upset them. Thus, parents are often unaware of the finer details of the children's suffering, although they can see that they are upset. There is often a great sense of frustration between parents and children at moments like this.

b. Not talking with peers After a few days, survivors may feel a great need to talk over their experiences with their peers. Unfortunately the timing is often inopportune. Peers hold back from asking in case they upset the survivor further; the survivor often feels rejected.

c. Foreshortened future and change of priorities Learning how easily life can be extinguished can cause young people to lose their faith in the future. They may feel that their whole view of the world, and their own priorities, have been altered. Many feel that they should live each day to the full and not plan ahead: they lose trust in long-term planning. Others realise that they have been over-concerned with materialistic or petty matters and resolve to re-think their values, sometimes within a formal religion.

d. Guilt 'Survivor guilt' has long been considered a paradoxical reaction following a disaster. Child and adolescent survivors often feel guilty that they are alive when others have died. They feel guilty that they could have done more to help others during the disaster. They sometimes also feel guilty about things they did during the crisis in order to survive.

(3) Heightened anxiety and arousal

In children and adolescents, heightened anxiety and arousal may appear as:

a. Concentration difficulties During the day children may have major problems concentrating on school work. For example, when it is silent in the classroom they may have intrusive memories of what happened to them.

b. Sleep disturbance Almost every young person involved in a disaster will have major sleep problems in the first few weeks. They report fears of the dark, fears of being alone, intrusive thoughts when things are quiet, bad dreams, nightmares and waking at intervals throughout the night. For some, these problems can persist over many months. Listening to music while dropping off to sleep can help divert distressing thoughts.

c. Separation difficulties Initially, most children want to be physically close to their surviving parents, often sleeping in the parental bed during the first few weeks. Some distressed parents find their children's clinginess difficult to cope with and many parents may find that they are irritated by this 'babyish' behaviour.

d. Memory problems Young people may have problems remembering new material or even old skills such as reading music.

e. Heightened alertness to dangers Survivors have learnt the
hard way that life is fragile. They become alert to all sorts of
dangers in the environment that they previously ignored. For
example, those who survive transport accidents are wary of all
forms of transport and are unwilling to put their safety in the hands
of other people. They may also be affected by reports of other
disasters.

f. Fears Most survivors of disasters are likely to develop fears
related to their experiences. Survivors of transport accidents may
develop fears of travelling by sea and air. Others have fears of
swimming, or the sound of rushing water. Children who are badly
mauled by dangerous dogs develop fears of other dogs and
animals. It is this spread of fears from an original threat to
something different that often prevents adults from spotting the
connection between the child's behaviour and the traumatic event.

g. Irritability Many children find themselves much more irritable
than previously, both with parents and peers. Some also find that
they get much more angry.

Many children also show other reactions and symptoms such as:

h. Depression Adolescents involved in disasters report
significantly higher rates of depression than do others of the same
age. Many adolescents experience fluctuations in their mood and,
understandably, such ups and downs may be worse after a
catastrophe. However, it is important to differentiate between
fluctuating low mood and persistent low mood coupled with
feelings of low self worth, loss of appetite and disrupted sleep. This
amounts to a clinical depression. A few adolescents also develop
suicidal thoughts and occasionally take overdoses.

i. Bereavement reactions When children have been bereaved by
an accident, no treatment plan can ignore the children's grief.
Bereavement reactions complicate the way other symptoms show
themselves but must be attended to. (See Further Reading in
Appendix 2)

j. Anxiety and panic A significant number of children become
very anxious after accidents, although the appearance of panic
attacks is sometimes considerably delayed. Usually it is possible to

identify stimuli in the child's immediate environment that trigger off panic attacks, hence the need to obtain as detailed an account as possible of the impact of the trauma on all the child's senses.

(4) Effects on younger children

Infants and pre-school children have been less systematically studied than older children and adults. In part this is because adults often avoid talking to the child about what happened hoping that they are too young to appreciate fully what happened to them. Even very young children can be keenly sensitive to their parents' distress and quickly learn not to talk about their bad experiences. However, it is possible to get children as young as four to six years old to describe vividly what they had experienced.

Very young children may show all sorts of regressive or anti-social behaviour. Children who have been dry at night may start wetting their beds again. Children who have slept in their own beds may need to sleep with their parents for a while. Children who have been well-adjusted and happy may become easily frustrated, irritable and destructive.

A number of the pre-school children who survived the sinking of the 'Herald of Free Enterprise' were reported by their parents and teachers as getting involved in repetitive play or drawings involving themes about the ship. One four year-old girl involved her playmates in endless games of nurses patching up the injured which went on for many months. A six year-old boy drew many pictures of 'the bad ferry' and spoke about it often in class with an understanding teacher. The day the head teacher took the class she forbade him talk to about it again. That night he began having nightmares and a few months later he tried to kill himself by poking a metal rod into an electric socket. He said he wanted to die to stop the pictures of the bad ferry in his head.

Three other pre-school boys became aggressive and anti-social both at home and at school. Their parents knew they were still upset thinking about the ferry, but they could never talk about it to anyone. When things got bad, the children would gouge out pieces of plaster or destroy toys or pick fights with other children.

Very young children have only limited understanding of the life-threatening nature of disasters. Even so, we know that some pre-school children also have very adult concepts of death and dying. It is important that we remember the range of individual differences in understanding when discussing (or not discussing) the effects of disasters with children. It is always a good strategy to get children to repeat to you what you have tried to explain. That way, any muddles or misunderstandings are quickly revealed and can be corrected.

As young children's understanding develops they will need to go back over the troubling events, to make better sense of them from a more advanced level of understanding.

(5) Effect on teachers

Teachers have to relate to all pupils, those involved in an incident and others. They also have to relate to the rest of the staff and to their own relatives and friends outside school. Teachers may also experience difficulty in knowing when to talk about the incident and when not to. If they have been involved in the crisis, they may develop problems in concentration and memory. Some may try working out their problems inappropriately. For example, they may sometimes seek out children to confide in, thereby adding to the children's burden. At other times, instead of discussing their difficulties with other teachers, they may discuss them in class with the children. Other staff need to be aware of this to ensure that appropriate help and support (see later) are available for teachers and other staff who are involved in major incidents.

To talk or not to talk?

When a personal tragedy befalls someone it is often difficult to know what best to do or say. Teachers in schools are in much the same dilemma - when should they talk about it to the young person? When should they leave well alone? There are no easy answers; but it is clear that not facing the dilemma can often make things worse.

For example, one party of school children returned from a trip abroad during which they were involved in a bloody terrorist attack. Fortunately no one in the party was killed. Although they came back to a blaze of publicity, a harassed senior member of staff thought the best thing to do was to try to pretend nothing had happened. In contrast to another group who had also been on a school journey at the same time, those involved in the attack were forbidden to put up pictures of their trip and were strongly discouraged from talking about their experiences. Offers of help from outside agencies were ignored. Three months later, survivors needed specialist help.

Who is most likely to be affected?

Sometimes it is immediately obvious when young people are affected by symptoms of PTSD. Certain symptoms, however, may take longer to surface. It is important, therefore, to know who are liable to be affected the most, so that teachers can keep an eye on those most likely to need help.

(1) Young people whose lives were at greatest risk are most likely to suffer emotional consequences

This is illustrated by the case of the sniper in the Californian school. Those children who were trapped in the line of fire in the playground suffered most, as judged by individual clinical assessments; those who were on the school premises, but not in direct danger, suffered to a medium extent; those not attending school that day (one third were out of school on planned rotation) were affected least. There were however exceptions to this. The little boy who went off to play football, leaving his sister in the playground, felt very guilty and suffered a great deal.

A similar gradation was found in one school where a party of 25 girls survived the 'Jupiter' sinking. It was considered that those girls who had asked to go on the cruise but were not awarded places would be more affected than those who never expressed an interest. And so it was found: there was a relationship between exposure and after effects with respect to measures of anxiety and depression. However, only the girls who experienced the sinking showed an increase in fears related to boats, drowning and the like.

(2) Those who witness death and carnage

Survivors of disasters are more adversely affected if the cause is technological or deliberate than if it is a natural disaster. Either way, children who see people badly injured or killed are likely to be more distressed.

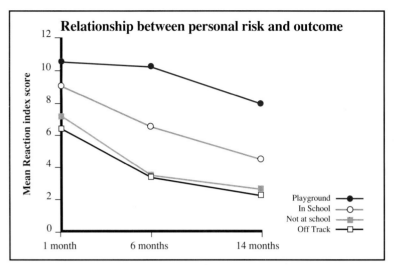

Nader K, Pynoos R S, Fairbanks I and Frederick C (1991) *Childhood PTSD reactions one year after a sniper attack, American Journal of Psychiatry,* 147, 1526-1530

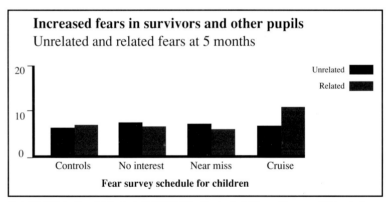

Yule W, Udwin O and Murdoch K (1990) *The 'Jupiter' sinking: effects on children's fears, depression and anxiety, Journal of Child Psychology and Psychiatry,* 31, 1051-1061

(3) Children who come from unstable family relationships

Although it is less well founded in empirical studies, children who are emotionally unstable or come from unstable family relationships are likely to suffer more and for longer than those in more supportive relationships.

(4) Children who are less able intellectually

Although it might be expected that more able children would be more affected by having a better understanding of all that had happened, current evidence suggests that it is the less able child who is more adversely affected.

(5) Gender differences

There is a higher proportion of problems among girls than among boys.

(6) Refugee children

Refugee children are often suffering from Post Traumatic Stress Disorder, culture shock *and* language difficulties. It is important to try to disentangle the three sets of responses. Recently several schools have developed excellent strategies to help children in similar positions. We refer to a useful book on this subject, in Further Reading, at the back of this book.

Schools cannot do anything about most of these risk factors, but if a disaster does strike, the factors can be used to identify children who should be monitored with especial care.

WHAT SCHOOLS CAN DO

Developing a contingency plan
New South Wales Department of School Education, Australia (March 1991)

School management teams and governors should develop a plan that involves the following steps:

1 Identifying Potential Critical Incidents
2 Identifying Support Agencies and Personnel
3 Developing a School Critical Incident Management Plan
4 Clarifying Roles - for all Personnel including Ancillary Staff

---

We have described how pupils and staff can be affected both emotionally and in their work achievements by crises, and that these effects can sometimes last for many years.

What can a school do to plan ahead to minimise the impact of such crises? How can it avoid making a 'drama out of a crisis'?

We now describe what schools are likely to face in the immediate, short, medium and long-term phases of a crisis. Each of these phases presents a variety of challenges that school managers will need to consider. We draw attention to the principal decisions, not always obvious, that have to be faced, and offer suggestions as to how the tasks should be assigned. We also consider the broader implications for curriculum planning. The section concludes with advice on developing a school contingency plan.

Immediate tasks

(1) The need for factual information

When a crisis occurs the first task is to obtain accurate information and to relay it to senior management within the school. Disasters happening away from school premises will be unclear for many hours, but there is still a need to convey as much accurate information as possible. Uncertainty breeds rumour, which adds to distress.

27

(2) Information out and in

After a fire that destroyed the science block in a
Cambridgeshire school, the deputy head was reported as
saying:

*"Communications were a top priority. The school's only
outside line was jammed with incoming calls, but we were
able to use another number in the community education
office. It is very important in a crisis to have a line
exclusively for outgoing calls." (Times Educational
Supplement* 24.1.92)

Where pupils have been involved in an accident outside the
school, the party leader needs to have an emergency number on
which to make contact with senior management back at school or
at their homes. This should be different from the regular school
number.

Some thought should also be given to the possibility of borrowing
a portable telephone for use by senior management to maintain
contact with the appropriate authority and the party leader. This
will enable the school to get on with its business while parents and
press are trying to phone in.

(3) Dealing with enquiries

The families of the young people caught in a tragedy will need full
and accurate information. They may need to be brought to the
school to receive it.

In the event of a tragedy, the school will be inundated with
telephone calls. This means that people will need to staff the
school switchboard which can be a stressful task dealing with
distressed and worried enquirers, especially when there is
uncertainty or bad news.

Those answering the phones should keep notes and have them
checked against school records so that there is certainty about who
has phoned in and who should still be contacted.

Schools should always have an up-to-date list of the pupils' next-
of-kin and where to make contact with them. When groups of

children and teachers go off the premises, a named member of staff still at school should have a copy of the list. Other members of staff should at least know where to find it. As soon as an incident is reported, in or out of school, parents and guardians should be informed and advised how further information will be conveyed and by whom.

(4) Informing parents

Parents need to be made contact with promptly but the speed will depend on the nature and scale of the disaster. This may be done in person or may have to be undertaken by telephone. Many schools already operate a 'telephone tree': some parents telephone others to make sure that accurate information is passed on more quickly.

Wherever possible, parents of all the other children in the school should be warned that the school has experienced a crisis and that their child may be upset.

It is difficult to give very specific advice here because of the many different ways crises occur, but there are some general pointers which will ensure that the information is passed on effectively and sensitively:

a. brief the member of staff making the contact, perhaps rehearsing the message first;

b. take careful note of those parents who still need to be informed so that those who already know are not made contact with unnecessarily;

c. offer help with the arrangement of transport;

d. check that the parents are not left alone in distress, perhaps making suggestions for making contact with relatives or neighbours;

e. offer useful phone numbers, either for support or for more information. For example, the emergency disaster number or the hospital number;

f. where appropriate, give the contact numbers of other families involved in the crisis.

(5) Dealing with the media

One of the tasks of schools must be to protect children, parents and staff from the glare of publicity, particularly during the first week or so. While the media can help inform the public responsibly, it can also be harmfully intrusive at times of stress and personal grief. Reporters move on to the next catastrophe; a survivor may live for years with a foolish quote in an unguarded moment.

A senior person on the staff should be nominated as press officer to deal with the media. It is not advisable to permit press and television on to the school premises or to give them access to staff or children unless there are specific reasons for doing so. All enquiries should be directed to and through the press officer who can arrange to have a briefing session with the press if necessary (ie journalists may be invited to a particular part of the school at a specified time). If the press are aware of these arrangements, they may be less inclined to crowd the school gates or try to interview individual pupils, staff or parents. While factual information may be given to the press, the privacy of staff, young people and their families should be maintained.

Members of staff dealing directly with families involved in the crisis should not be asked to take on the task of dealing with the press as well. It may be possible to get a person seconded from the appropriate authority to act as press officer.

(6) Informing the staff

As soon as an incident is confirmed, the senior management team needs to meet to decide their strategies. This group should appoint a small team (eg the class teacher, deputy head, home/school liaison teacher), relieve them of other duties, and allow them to manage the crisis over the next few hours. Some of the tasks facing that team will already have been thought through and need only to be activated, but the nature of the incident and the immediate availability of staff may require some adjustment.

The rest of the staff should be informed as soon as possible, preferably at a specially convened staff meeting. Again it is essential that both teaching staff and ancillary staff share the same information so that untrue rumours do not circulate.

(7) Informing the pupils

Pupils should be told simply and without fabrication what has happened. It is probably best if this is done in the smallest groups possible - their classes, their year groups, tutor groups or however the school is organised. Their questions should be answered as straightforwardly as possible. Staff who undertake this task should be told to pass on facts only and never to speculate on the causes of the crisis or its consequences. Where questions cannot be answered at the time, this should be acknowledged.

If a school is to close, children and parents should be told by the end of the school day, preferably at the same time as parents are told about the incident. Closure should, on the whole, be avoided.

(8) Stick to a normal routine

As far as possible the school's normal routine should be followed. This is to ensure some security in the lives of the pupils at a time of crisis.

(9) Inform governors and the appropriate authority

The chair of governors, the chief education officer and other appropriate officers of the authority should be informed as soon as possible after a major incident so that previously agreed assistance can be given.

(10) Attendance at funerals

People from differing backgrounds and religions have different burial rites. Some, including Parsees, Sikhs and Jews, may hold funerals within 24 hours of death. There is not always time therefore to prepare staff and pupils for attendance. In this case a member of staff should swiftly make enquiries about the burial customs (for example, if flowers are in order and whether women and men and representatives from the school - including pupils - would be welcome).

Summary

- Ensure that accurate information can get into and out of the school
- Ensure that several staff have access to next-of-kin lists
- Set up strategies for dealing with enquiries
- Inform (with care and sensitivity) parents
- Choose a member of staff to deal with the media
- Inform staff and pupils in an appropriate and careful way
- Attempt to stick to normal school routines
- Inform the governors and appropriate authority
- Make plans for attendance at funerals

Short-term action

Once it is confirmed that the school is facing a major crisis, staff and pupils may feel shocked and numbed as well as under strong pressure to talk. Head teachers and staff will face a number of decisions. If they understand normal reactions to disaster, these decisions will be more appropriately informed.

(1) Re-uniting children with their parents

If a disaster happens outside school it is essential to ensure the physical safety of all the children - to obtain whatever first aid or other medical help is needed - and then to inform their parents. Generally, it is important that children should be re-united with their families as soon as practicable.

While in most instances children should be brought home, sometimes the parents may need to be taken to the children, and also to the scene of the accident: parents, appreciating the circumstances and the location of the accident, will be better able to share this later with their children. Children may get a different view of the scene of the accident in the presence of their parent(s); in consequence they may develop fewer fears.

(2) Managing the staff

A whole school is involved in a tragedy even though some may be more affected than others. The burden of coping with the crisis should not be allowed to fall on only one or two staff, however willing and dedicated. All staff, both teaching and support, will need an opportunity to express their emotional reactions to the crisis. Support should be organised, as far as possible, from within the school itself. It may be that one member of staff, who is more comfortable than the others when talking about feelings, could arrange to be accessible to those who need support. The same member of staff may set up a regular support group for staff in which they can talk about their reactions. If no member of staff feels confident in doing this work then a reliable agency outside the school could be approached (see later).

Senior staff need to protect their colleagues from over-working. People need to have some rest: others have to ensure that the senior staff follow their own advice. It is important that the co-ordinator is aware of the length of duties and makes sure that regular relief and debriefing are given. Even if senior staff do not feel able to offer counselling support to other staff, they can make sure that it is available. Tired and upset staff will not be able to make sensible decisions if the crisis persists over many hours.

(3) Giving staff 'permission' to talk

After a major trauma staff need to know that it is perfectly natural to want to talk about the incident and to share their feelings. It is important, however, to distinguish between the continual rehearsing of the incident that shows that some may need more professional help than schools can usually offer, and those who need space and time to talk before getting on with their lives.

(4) Making contact with outside professionals

This is the point at which to refer to the list of contacts in the contingency plan. It is hoped that the time spent developing the links will now reveal that the contacts outside the school are reliable and fit the way the school wishes to work. As soon as practicable, arrangements should be made for formal help to be available within the school - whether from specially chosen teaching staff or from outside mental health professionals. The role of the psychologists, psychiatrists, social workers, counsellors or volunteers should be to support the efforts of the staff, not to replace them.

Contact should be made, where appropriate, with local religious and community leaders who can advise on funeral and mourning rites, who can support the families during this time, and who could perhaps be invited into an assembly to talk to the whole school about issues previously agreed. Some voluntary agencies such as Cruse and the Samaritans may also be able to offer helpful guidance for dealing with death and mourning.

At such a time of crisis there may be many offers of help from outside the school. It may be difficult to know when to say 'yes' and when to say 'no' and whom to work with. Before accepting offers of help, head teachers should check on the experience and qualifications of the people concerned. They could do this by checking the social, medical and psychological services they have already vetted on the contact list in Appendix 1.

The head teacher has legal responsibility for what happens to the pupils in school. When the head teacher invites help and advice from professionals outside, this is done by creating a partnership. The head teacher has the right to decide who has access to the children in school. They are entitled to clarify what arrangements are to be made for imparting information. Referring children to other agencies does not mean handing over all responsibility for them.

(5) Encouraging pupils to talk

After a disaster pupils as well as staff may feel an enormous pressure to talk about their experiences. After a few days this can become irritating for those young people who were not involved. Initially adults should listen, no matter how disruptive it is to the task in hand; after a few days the young people should be encouraged to talk to a designated member of staff, although the young people themselves should obviously have some say in the choice of listener.

Adolescents, and in particular boys, may have difficulty sharing their emotional reactions with parents, peers and teachers alike. Teaching staff should recognise that whatever formal, pastoral care is already in place, they should capitalise on any informal, personal support network. They need to be aware of the trauma, be prepared to talk and to listen. They will need to make themselves more available than usual. Inexperienced staff may get overwhelmed by the young people's distress and should, in that event, seek advice from more experienced colleagues.

As always, it is important to observe and to **listen to** the child. A perceptive teacher is not intrusive, and knows when to talk and when to listen. When a child looks distressed or, uncharacteristically, has gone quiet over several days, then the perceptive teacher may take that child aside and ask what he or she is feeling. Experience has shown that children will not talk about their innermost feelings to parents and teachers unless they are given strong signals that it is safe to do so. Plenty of time must be allowed once the child starts to unburden. A word of warning, however - teachers need to obtain 'permission' from the child to talk this way.

Children quickly read the cues when adults do not wish to get involved. Their subsequent silence should not be taken as evidence of lack of suffering.

(6) Remembering the event

Sensitivity is required in gauging whether young people want to talk about their experiences, or whether they would prefer to keep them to themselves, especially if they do not feel 'safe' and at ease with other young people around. It often helps children to express whatever has happened to them through mime, dance, writing, drawing or other art forms. Many may do this spontaneously. Very young children, for example, may choose to draw. In the immediate aftermath it can be helpful to allocate time for this and to share the stories or poems or drawings that children may produce. The teacher needs to be aware that in doing so children may get upset, but equally that such distress can be healing.

(7) Helping the rest of the class or the school to come to terms with the crisis

Other pupils in the school may need some education about 'normal' stress reactions and the need not just for immediate sympathy, but longer-term understanding.

Many young people who have not been directly involved in the incident may need to find ways of working through their own distress, particularly if they were close to someone involved in the crisis. Opportunities can be created for the whole class to support the distressed child, and to alleviate their own distress. If the young person in question is at home or in hospital the class could think of ways of showing their support, such as writing and sending cards, videos, or audio tapes. If the child is present and wants to talk about the incident, especially where deaths may have occurred, the class could discuss memorials such as photographs or flowers.

(8) Individual differences in adjustment

Children and staff may respond to a crisis in different ways and at a different paces. For example, not every child will be ready to make a drawing of the accident or write about it. Teachers and other staff will need to be sensitive to such individual differences otherwise more harm than good may be done.

(9) Reactions of younger children

Younger children may incorporate features of the accident into their play. For them this may be the equivalent of having repetitive images or dreams and may well be a way of their gaining control over their lives. The play should be noted and allowed, provided always that it is not upsetting or interfering with others. It is not a sign of ghoulish obsession with death or carnage. Teachers and other staff such as playtime supervisors may be less upset by such activities once they realise that they may well serve a healthy purpose.

(10) Monitoring the effects

Many of the most distressing effects of major traumas are subjective and internal. It is not always possible tell by looking at a survivor if he or she is having constant video-like replays of the events. Spotting that children are concentrating less well than usual, or that their work is deteriorating or that they look tired and upset, is a skill. Strategies such as asking friends to look for signs of distress, reminding class teachers and form tutors to be alert to the potential signs, and talking with parents more regularly than usual about the young person's state in the classroom, are all ways of keeping an eye on their well-being.

(11) A debriefing meeting

Many people recommend that there should be a formal meeting to 'debrief' all those involved, both staff and children. Such a meeting may serve a number of important purposes. For example, it may:

a. Clarify what happened
b. Allow for a sharing of reactions
c. Reassure the participants that such reactions are not abnormal
d. Mobilise resources

During a major trauma, people are often numbed. They feel as if things are not really happening to them. For a few days after the event they are often in a state of shock. Thereafter, upset as they may be, it is important that someone helps them to begin to make sense of what actually happened. Debriefing is a way of talking about not only what happened, but of sharing the often frightening emotional reactions to the events. By holding a debriefing meeting in the school, usually led by an experienced person from outside, the school is giving the pupils and staff permission to exchange their reactions and educating them in how best to cope in the period that follows. A separate debriefing meeting may be necessary for staff who are directly affected by the crisis.

(12) Expressing sympathy

In the chaos that can follow a major incident it is important to express sympathy to those families and children and staff who have been hurt or bereaved. Not only should someone from school visit the injured in hospital but other children should be encouraged to send them cards and messages. The school also needs to think about sending a representative to funerals.

Summary

- Organise reunion of children with parents
- Activate those on the list of outside contacts
- Arrange briefing meeting for staff
- Arrange debriefing meeting for directly affected staff
- Check that procedures for monitoring staff and pupils are in place
- Activate strategies for allowing young people to express their feelings about the situation, if they wish
- Contact families of those hurt or bereaved and express sympathy

Medium-term action

As the school settles into its normal routine after a few days, staff and pupils will begin to realise more clearly what has happened to them. The initial period of numbness may give way to a period of more public expressions of distress. While schools will want to maintain as normal a routine as possible, some alterations will be inevitable. For example, decisions about continuing the monitoring of pupils, referring for specialist help, and attending funerals or memorial services may have to be taken. We describe below some other tasks that may arise.

(1) Helping people to come back into school

Some schools already have careful plans for welcoming and phasing in children after long absences or illnesses. These plans include negotiating with both the young people and their parents a date for returning; planning with teachers the actual entry into lessons, including the possibility of part-time attendance at first; developing feasible plans of work; briefing classmates and identifying particular teachers and children to provide the closest support.

Although young people often worry about the work they have missed, staff should ensure that re-entry into school is not just about catching up with work - it is also about meeting friends and beginning to get back to normal. If necessary, the missed work can be left undone because getting the child back into school may be the priority.

Sometimes young people who are trying to recover away from school welcome school work at home. Their re-entry into school may not be so daunting if their backlog of undone work is decreased, either by the teacher giving permission not to do it, or helping a pupil to catch up on the most important pieces of work, or by the work being done at home. A home visit from teachers may be the first step towards re-entry; friends may want to arrange a rota of visits with the intention of keeping them informed of daily events in school, including some of the assignments they have had.

It may help re-entry if discussions are held about planning the actual moment with the rest of the class. Some classes may want to discuss what to say by way of welcome, and some young people coming back into school may wish to know what information has been given about them to their class.

Some young people may be coming back into school having sustained injuries which have changed them physically in some way. For example, they may have scars, they may have had limbs amputated, they may limp, they may have lost their hair, or they may have gained or lost considerable amounts of weight. Re-entry can be very difficult for these people, particularly if they are caught up in the self-consciousness of adolescence. The change in their self-image may well be much greater than the visible signs of the injuries. A discussion with them about what to say to the rest of the class may ease their re-entry and allay some fears. It should also be possible to help them evolve strategies to deal with the teasing that may come from people who have not been part of the preparation for their return.

As part of the contingency plan we suggest that schools review their strategies for easing young people's re-entry into school after a prolonged absence or illness. This list could include:

a. A form teacher visiting a pupil at home or in hospital

b. Making a decision about how to maintain contact with school and who should do this

c. Checking whether any work or books have been lost in the incident; if so, making a decision about replacements

d. Checking what worries there are about public examinations; if there are any, considering special arrangements with examining boards. This is easily done. There are formal mechanisms with each examination board which are triggered by a letter from the school

e. Considering part-time attendance and deciding on a suitable curriculum within a realistic time span

f. Checking on worries about meeting other pupils and discussing how to react to questions and comments

g. Setting up 'sanctuary' arrangements for the young person to go to in school should he or she get particularly upset

h. Talking about what is happening in school, both generally and specifically, including reactions to the incident

i. Re-scheduling projects and other work in so far as it is necessary and possible

(2) Exploring alternative teaching methods

On coming back into school, concentration, or even the physical activity of writing, may be very difficult. If one teacher has been instrumental in negotiating the re-entry into school, that teacher will know what expectations other teachers may have of the young person. Everyone involved should then be clearly informed.

(3) Specialist support for the staff

The aim of the work done (in the school and the classroom, as well as any specialist work done in groups or individually) is the same - to enable pupils and staff to adapt. In particular the aim is to help them cope with what happened, rather than to undermine their coping strategies. It may be that a school has made a decision in its contingency plan to ask a consultant to work indirectly with the staff and children by helping them to understand and encourage the development of coping strategies. This might mean talking to other people who will then work with the staff.

A clear distinction needs to be made between outside support organised for the teachers to help them with their own reactions, and support arranged for the children to be mediated through the teachers. Staff needs may be pressing and require attention, but sessions set up by specialists to help staff to help children should not be hijacked to deal with staff members' own difficulties.

(4) Staff supporting the children

Children can be taught to develop effective coping strategies such as the ability to relax when they feel tense or anxious. They can be helped to make sense of what happened and to understand that, even though they may feel guilty, they are not to blame. Children can be helped to cope with feelings of being overwhelmed. They can be helped to acc-ept that temporarily they cannot do as much as they did before and to realise that they will need to take things at an easier pace than before.

Teachers should take every opportunity to praise children for using these techniques. Children who admit to having difficulty with concentration should be praised for recognising this rather than battling on; then they can be helped to work out a realistic work schedule.

(5) Specialist treatment for the children

Where the school chooses to have an outside consultant (such as a psychologist, social worker, counsellor or psychiatrist) to advise staff on how to help the children, a few ground rules need to be agreed to avoid misunderstandings.

Some ground rules to observe when working with outside consultants

- Children, staff and the consultant should agree the boundaries of sharing confidential information. Many medical and non-medical therapists, particularly those trained in individual psychodynamic therapies, are used to maintaining complete confidentiality between therapist and child. This is not appropriate when staff are being helped to help the child. Equally, it is not appropriate to share all information with everyone. Adolescents may feel particularly strongly about what information is to be shared with their parents or with teachers. Staff need to keep to a minimum the information they share about a pupil. Pupils should never be given a promise that all information will be kept secret.

- Staff should be clear about whom to make contact with when they are worried about a particular child.

- Regular meetings between the consultant and appropriate staff will enable progress to be reviewed and the consultant to suggest ways in which the school can continue to offer support.

One question that working with health, social work, psychological or educational specialists invites is: who has overall responsibility and control for what happens in school? The answer is that this remains with the head teacher. The normal ground rules, clarified in the Children Act of 1989, apply: schools cannot take unilateral decisions about help for children without the permission of parents and of the older pupils themselves.

Part of the planned approach may involve calling in some of these other professionals to run groups in schools. These groups will aim to boost the children's coping skills, educate them further about the ways disasters may affect them, train them in relaxation techniques to help reduce anxiety and promote better sleep patterns, suggest techniques to help them gradually expose themselves to the situation they have been avoiding, allow them to discuss feelings of guilt for things done or not done during the disaster, and so on.

Therapists will probably want to work closely with teaching staff and keep them informed of progress. It may be to everyone's benefit that teachers and young people use the therapists as go-betweens to negotiate such issues as attendance and work. Therapists need to make sure that they do not usurp the pastoral role of staff, but strengthen and support it. Teachers will be there long after the specialists have left and it is important that they do not feel de-skilled as a result of the specialists' relationships with pupils.

Some children will not want to participate in formal treatment groups within the school nor even use teachers as confidants: they or their families may want individual help. Individual therapy will resemble group work, but will be more intense. There will need to be clear procedures for referring children for individual help, or for ensuring that families have arranged for this. Negotiations about the flow of necessary information are important here - for example, when the outside treatment is coming to a close, the school will need to know this. The school and the agency need to get together to agree common strategies for dealing with subsequent problems: how to monitor the child(ren); what to expect and how to maintain contact. For example, lists of specialists and their addresses should be available to staff, parents and pupils alike, in case they wish to seek help at a later date.

(6) Attendance at funerals

There are many different religious and cultural views about the participation of young people in funeral rites. The school will want to respect these views and customs as well as the wishes of parents and the children themselves.

The current consensus among mental health professionals is that most children (and adults) come to terms with their grief more quickly if they say farewell formally. Whenever possible, survivors should be encouraged and enabled to attend the funerals of those who died, and the parents of those who died should be encouraged to allow it.

(7) Special assemblies and memorial services

In addition to funerals that families may choose to be private, schools may wish to mark the event with a special assembly or a memorial service. Discussions could be held with staff, governors, parents, pupils and the local community on what form this should take and who should be involved. Planning the ceremony often becomes an important therapeutic act in itself.

For many who have been affected by a major incident, a memorial service acts as a way of acknowledging that it is now over. Even so, many staff and pupils may be upset during the service and this needs to be considered in planning, for example, where it is to be held and if access should be given to the media. Some schools have planted special gardens in memory of pupils or staff members, others have installed seats in the playground in their memory or have commissioned sculptures or paintings.

(8) Keeping families informed

Remember to keep families informed. Information sheets for families can be useful. The information could include:

a. who has been called in to advise staff and pupils

b. how parents can have access to help

c. whom to make contact with if they are worried about their child's progress

(9) Continued monitoring of children's progress

By now staff and parents should know the person to whom to report any concerns about a child. Pupils too should be clear about whom to talk to. Some staff will be meeting regularly, occasionally with an outside consultant, and part of the agenda should be to keep children under review. Records should be kept and children referred as necessary. It should be made clear that records held in the schools are open to inspection by parents and older pupils. Guidelines should be established on how to maintain contact with parents: for example, a short letter home might draw attention to the progress made by pupils in their return to 'normality'.

The parents of children in any of the high risk groups described earlier should be given the option of receiving specialist help. If the children's distress remains high six to eight weeks after the incident, they should be referred to a specialist with skills in treating PTSD. Staff and parents need to be clear about the procedures for ensuring appropriate help quickly.

Summary

- Ensure a member of staff makes contact with children at home or in hospital
- Make sensitive arrangements for the return to school
- Arrange alternative teaching if necessary
- Arrange support for affected staff
- Arrange consultation so staff can better support children
- Ensure clear understanding of consultation, especially its confidentiality
- Clarify procedures for referring children for individual help
- Liaise with parents, to include the sending of bulletins
- Decide about attendance at funerals
- Share the planning of the special assembly or memorial service
- Check that monitoring procedures are in place and followed

Longer-term planning

However painful and stressful, traumatic events often provide opportunities for reappraisal, sometimes of practice and more especially of attitudes and values. Tragedies can bring people together. In schools the experience can be so profound that staff want to retain the sense of community that the event has generated. Schools should remember that the effects of a crisis can reverberate for years. In this section we highlight some of the more predictable issues that merit consideration.

(1) Keeping an eye on vulnerable people

It is difficult to keep the memory of events alive as schools are absorbed by their day-to-day affairs. A school may consider devising a system of record-keeping in which information on such a disaster is recorded. It is important that new staff and staff new to vulnerable children are briefed on the most helpful way of continuing to support the children of a disaster as recorded in the system.

(2) Marking anniversaries

Anniversaries are often difficult times. It is better if decisions about how to treat anniversaries are made collectively in good time before the anniversary. These decisions could include an annual memorial prize; the planting of a special garden that blooms at the appropriate time; a commemorative assembly or concert. Decisions must obviously take account of the wishes and feelings of the parents of pupils who were maimed or killed.

(3) Legal processes

The legal processes after a disaster, such as inquests, boards of enquiry, postponed funerals and court appearances, can interfere with mourning. They can prolong or impede it, or even begin it again as a new legal process commences. Schools, both in their record-keeping and in their general vigilance, need to be aware when members of the school are involved in these legal processes.

(4) The story changes

Part of the normal process of mourning is trying, repeatedly, to understand what happened and why. Guilt and blame are apportioned, and enormously uncomfortable feelings are aroused. Often during official enquiries long afterwards, the story is pieced together and re-told. History is re-written. Explanations, guilt and blame are re-distributed, and those people most closely connected with the tragedy may be left with deeply distressing feelings which differ from those they felt just after the event.

Schools need to be aware when these stories are being re-told, and to be ready, if necessary, with the emotional support that was originally available.

Summary

- Introduce strategies to continue monitoring vulnerable pupils and staff
- Consult and decide on whether and how to mark anniversaries
- Ensure that new staff are aware of which pupils were affected, and in what way, and that they know how to obtain further help if necessary
- Remember that legal processes, enquiries and even news stories may bring back distressing memories and cause temporary upset within the school

Implications for the curriculum

We noted early on that some schools respond better at times of crisis than others. Many schools have coped well with dreadful crises and, for them, much of what we have said will be obvious. They may not have been fully aware of the effects of crises on the children, but they have had carefully thought-through procedures in place and have been able to put them into practice effectively.

Here we want to draw attention to some implications for curriculum planning: to what is taught and how schools tackle sensitive issues such as death and injury. We choose to write about 'curriculum planning' because we think that schools should not have to deal with such enormously difficult issues as death and bereavement for the first time after a disaster. The appearance of these issues in the curriculum will mean that pupils will already have had some familiarity with them, even if only in the classroom. Whatever the age of the children, the issues can be embedded in the curriculum, so that the young people are used to talking about such subjects. In this way they will not be shrouded in mystery and taboo. As with the development and implementation of sex education policies, parents and governors can be involved in the planning.

(1) Dealing with sensitive issues within the curriculum

The curriculum of some schools includes looking at life, death, bereavement and other rites of passage within a multi-cultural and multi-faith framework. These issues are often explored through well-chosen literature in RE, drama, history, humanities and sociology. Primary schools often include such issues in projects about self, health or families. Some secondary schools explore subjects such as death and bereavement through the pastoral co-ordinators. Wherever a school chooses to refer to life, death and bereavement within the curriculum, they should not be dealt with simply as topics to be covered. In our Further Reading section there are some suggestions for teachers which may be of help.

(2) Helping teachers to deal with sensitive issues

Some teachers find it uncomfortable to explore ideas and feelings they are not completely at ease with. Increasingly, schools include staff development sessions for dealing with difficult feelings. These sessions may include specialist consultants working with small groups of teachers to help them address uncomfortable feelings and develop strategies for dealing with them, both for themselves and for the young people they work with.

(3) Multi-cultural and multi-faith issues

Schools need to be aware of their pupils' backgrounds. This includes having an informed understanding of different cultural and religious attitudes to disability, disasters, death, bereavement, mourning and funerals. Such awareness of diverse views and expectations contributes towards creating a supportive ethos within the school.

(4) Attributing blame

It is now reasonably well established that the explanations people give on the cause of any disaster can influence the speed with which those involved adjust. People who feel guilty for having somehow caused the accident generally take longer to recover. Schools should know their pupils and be aware of how different religious and ethnic groupings may interpret the causes of disaster. Such knowledge will be invaluable to all those, teaching staff and outside professionals, who are trying to help the children make sense of what happened.

(5) Social support

In general, people who feel socially supported in relationships where they can confide their feelings survive all sorts of tribulations better. Thus a school able to promote such an atmosphere of support, trust and confiding among its staff and pupils will be better able to cope with a disaster.

Summary

- Plan the curriculum to work with 'rites of passage' as a matter of course
- Set up strategies to support teachers when working with painful emotions and sensitive subjects
- Be aware of multi-cultural and multi-faith issues
- Remember that inevitably blame gets attributed
- Develop strategies for increasing social support between staff and between pupils

In the Further Reading and Useful Addresses sections there are suggestions to help schools work with the ideas in this section. The most useful suggestion, however, is that schools should recognise that they need to develop procedures for working with difficult feelings and painful emotions. Having made that decision, they will begin to deal with those feelings.

Developing a contingency plan

All that we have said points to the need for planning. Here we attempt to set out what contingency planning involves and what such a plan should look like. Although the development of this plan may initially seem time-consuming, it is important that all members of staff in a school understand that they are part of it. It is worth devoting a staff meeting or part of a staff development session to its formation. In the event of a crisis staff will be more able to move into action without having to waste time making decisions, and without having to wait for clarification about tasks to be done.

We suggest that a member of the senior management team is nominated to review and up-date the plan annually and to make it easily accessible to all members of staff.

The plan should include:

(1) The identification of potential crises

In the early part of this publication we listed a number of examples of disasters that might occur in your school. In developing your plan you may want to identify others that are likely to occur:

a. Death of a pupil or teacher
b. Violence and assault in school
c. Destruction or vandalism of part of school
d. Pupil or teacher being taken hostage
e. Road, sea or air traffic accident involving pupils
f. Natural disaster in the community
g. Death or injuries on school journeys
h. Civil disturbances and terrorism

(2) Choosing suitable support agencies and personnel

The list of significant contacts and telephone numbers will entail research, but the time involved will be worthwhile should an emergency arise. Personal contact with specialist services will make it more likely that there is mutual respect for expertise and assistance, and working relationships will not have to be established from scratch in a time of crisis. It also a good idea to establish which contacts will be more helpful than others.

In Appendix 1 we have suggested some of the people who might be suitable for the list. The list of contacts will vary according to the location of the school and the involvement of the school in the local community. We have designed the list so that phone numbers and relevant addresses can be added.

(3) Actions planned and responsibilities apportioned so that in the case of a crisis the whole operation moves as smoothly as possible to avoid delay and further harm

Within the school assign responsibility for the following tasks:

	Task	Time-scale
1	Obtain factual information at start of crisis	within hours
2	Senior management meet with support personnel	within hours
3	Establish an intervention team	within hours
4	Contact families	within hours: continue until all informed
5	Call a staff meeting to give information	same day if practicable
6	Inform pupils in small groups	same day if practicable
7	Arrange a debriefing meeting for staff involved in disaster	same day if practicable
8	Debriefing for pupils involved in the disaster	as soon as possible, allowing for health and safety
9	Identify high risk pupils and staff	next few days
10	Promote discussion in classes	next few days and weeks
11	Identify the need for group or individual treatment	incrementally over days or weeks after disaster
12	Organise treatment, etc	as required

Appendix 1: Useful Contacts

As part of the contingency plan this list of contacts should be obtained as a matter of course. Their phone numbers can be added to this page and the whole list can be attached to the staff notice board or the school handbook, and regularly updated. Office support staff should also have such a list readily available:

Contact	Name	Phone number
Director of Education		
Chair of Governing Body		
Police		
Fire Brigade		
School Doctor/Community Medical Officer		
School Nurse		
Educational Psychologist		
Child Guidance Clinic		
Child/Family Psychiatry Service		
Clinical Child Psychologist		
Emergency Department at the Local Hospital		
Home School Liaison Officer		
Education Social Worker		
Social Services Area Team Leader		

Counselling Services

Local Religious Groups

Other Voluntary Agencies

Press and Media Contacts

This list was updated on   /   / 19

This list was updated on   /   / 19

This list was updated on   /   / 19

Appendix 2: Further Reading

Ayalon, O (1988) *Rescue! Community oriented preventative education for coping with stress* Haifa: Nord Publications

Disasters Working Party (1991) *Disasters: planning for a caring response* London: HMSO

Dyregrov, A (1988) 'Critical incident stress debriefings' Research Centre for Occupational Health and Safety: University of Bergen, Norway

Gatliffe, E (1988) *Death in the Classroom - a resource book for teachers and others* London: Epworth Press

Hodgkinson, P E and Stewart, M (1991) *Coping with Catastrophe: a handbook of disaster management* London: Routledge

Hopson, B and Scally, M (1981) *Lifeskills Teaching Programmes - No 1*, Lifeskills Associates, Leeds

Johnson, Kendall (1989) *Trauma in the Lives of Children* Basingstoke: Macmillan

Lacey, G N (1972) 'Observations on Aberfan' *Journal of Psychosomatic Research*, Vol 16, 257-260

Lott, P (1989) *Out of School: a practical guide to the responsibilities of teachers in charge of school journeys* (4th edition) AMMA

Melzak, Sheila (1992) *Integrating Refugee Children Into Schools*, Minority Rights Group and Medical Foundation for the Care of the Tortured.

Mitchell, J (1993) 'When disaster strikes...the critical incident stress debriefing process' *Journal of Emergency Medical Services*, 8, 36-39

National Union of Teachers (1989 revised edition) *Beyond the Classroom: guidance from the NUT on school visits and journeys*

New South Wales Department of School Education (1990) *Management of Critical Incidents - a guide for schools* NSW Department of School Education, South Coast Region, PO Box 1232, Wollongong, NSW, Australia

Parry, Glenys (1990) *Coping with Crises*, British Psychological Society and Routledge

Perkins, G and Morris, L (1991) *Remembering Mum* London: A & C Black

Plant, S and Stoate, P (1989) *Loss and Change - resources for use in a personal and social education programme* Oxford: Pergamon Educational Press

Pynoos, R and Nader, K (1988) 'Psychological first aid and treatment approach for children exposed to community violence: research implications' *Journal of Traumatic Stress*, 1, 243-267

Raphael, B (1986) *When Disaster Strikes* London: Hutchinson

Wagner, Patsy (1993) *Children and Bereavement, Death and Loss: what can the school do?* Available: NAPCE Base, c/o Education Dept, University of Warwick, Coventry, CV4 7AL Tel: 0203 523810

Wagner, Patsy 'Schools and pupils: developing their responses to bereavement' in *Pastoral Care and PSE; Entitlement and Provision* (1993) eds R Best, P Lang, C Lodge and C Watkins, Cassell

Wallbank, Susan (1991) *Facing Grief - bereavement and the young adult* Cambridge: Lutterworth Press

Ward, B and Associates (1989) *Good Grief - exploring feelings, loss and death with under 11's - a holistic approach*, Good Grief, Grimstone Manor Mews, Yelverton, PL20 7QY

Ward, B and Associates (1988) *Good Grief for Secondary Age, FE and Adults*, Good Grief, Grimstone Manor Mews, Yelverton, PL20 7QY

Yule, W, Udwin, O and Murdoch, K (1990) 'The 'Jupiter' sinking: effects on children's fears, depression and anxiety' *Journal of Child Psychology and Psychiatry*, 31, 1051-1061

Yule, W (1991) 'Work with children following disasters' chapter in M Herbert (ed) *Clinical Child Psychology: social learning, development and behaviour* Chichester: John Wiley

Yule, W and Udwin, O (1991) 'Screening child survivors for post traumatic stress disorders: experiences from the 'Jupiter' sinking' *British Journal of Clinical Psychology*, 30, 131-138

Yule, W 'Post traumatic stress disorder' (1993) in Rutter, M, Hersov L and Taylor E (eds) *Child and adolescent psychiatry: modern approaches* (3rd edition) Oxford: Blackwells

Appendix 3: Useful Addresses

Dr Dora Black
Stress Clinic
Department of Child and Adolescent
Psychiatry
Royal Free Hospital
Pond Street
LONDON NW3 2OG
Tel: 071 794 6874

The British Red Cross
9 Grosvenor Crescent
LONDON SW1X 7EJ
Tel: 071 235 5454
*They have a useful leaflet on coping with
stress in a major crisis.*

**Centre for Crisis Management and
Education**
Elizabeth Capewell
93 Old Newton Road
NEWBURY RG14 7DE
Tel: 0635 30644

CRUSE - Bereavement Care
126 Sheen Road
RICHMOND
Surrey TW9 1UR
Tel: 081 940 4818

Good Grief
c/o Barbara Ward
3 Wheelwright Court
WALKHAMPTON PL20 6LA
Tel: 0822 855 619

**Medical Foundation for the Care of
Victims of Torture**
96 Grafton Road
LONDON NW5 3EJ
Tel: 071 284 4321

The Minority Rights Group
379 Brixton Road
LONDON SW9 7DE
Tel: 071 978 9498

**National Association for Pastoral Care in
Education**
c/o Department of Education
University of Warwick
COVENTRY CV4 7AL
Tel: 0203 523523

The Refugee Council
Bondway House
3 Bondway
LONDON SW8 1SJ
Tel: 071 582 6922

Samaritans
17 Uxbridge Road
SLOUGH
Berks SL1 1SN
Tel: 0753 32713

Dr James Thompson
Stress Clinic
Academic Department of Psychiatry
University College and Middlesex Hospital
School of Medicine
Ridinghouse Street
LONDON W1N 8AA
Tel: 071 380 9475

Victim Support Schemes Organisation
Cranmer House
39 Brixton Road
LONDON SW9 6DZ
Tel: 071 735 9166

Patsy Wagner
Deputy Principal Educational Psychologist
The Royal Borough of Kensington and
Chelsea
Professional Development Centre
108a Lancaster Road
LONDON W11 1QS
*Work on children and families, death and
loss - what schools can do. See also
Further Reading, Appendix 2.*

Professor William Yule
Traumatic Stress Clinic
Maudsley Hospital
Denmark Hill
LONDON SE5 9AF
Tel: 071 703 5411
See also Further Reading, Appendix 2.

Below are some education books published by the Foundation. A complete booklist is available free from Calouste Gulbenkian Foundation, 98 Portland Place, London W1N 4ET. Tel: 071 636-5313

The Arts in Schools: principles, practice and provision, edited by Professor Kenneth Robinson (1982, with new introduction 1989)

Over 20,000 copies sold. "...it should be not merely placed but forced into the hands of all heads, governors and administrators...The book bristles with practical organisational suggestions, most of which depend more on the exercise of ingenuity and imagination than on large amounts of cash." *Times Educational Supplement*

Parents in Secondary Education: the parent organiser project at Westminster City School by Berry Mayall

This school was the first in the UK to appoint a paid parent organiser to develop the involvement of parents in the work of the school.

Moving Culture: an enquiry into the cultural activities of young people by Paul Willis

"No one should dismiss the behaviour of the young as trivial, chaotic or meaningless before they have read this book." *Young People Now*

Artists in Wigan Schools by Rod Taylor

"An absorbing book, stunningly illustrated...put it on the required reading list not just of art and design teachers, but heads and administrators too." *Times Educational Supplement*

Vandalism and Graffiti: the state of the art by Frank Coffield

This looks at the reality behind vandalism, stripping away the myths, and discusses what can be done to reduce it.

"...contains more detailed proposals than anything else put forward in more than 20 years." *The Times*

Bullying: a child's view by Jean La Fontaine

An analysis of telephone calls from children to ChildLine about being bullied.

"This research should be used by every school in the country, primary and secondary: it is a realistic, sympathetic and constructive curriculum-planning tool." *The Guardian*. Copies of this book were mailed to every school in 1992.